D0651498

MAY 24 2021

the fire
never goes out

392 9090

The Fire Never Goes Out
Copyright © 2020 by Noelle Stevenson
All rights reserved. Manufactured in the United States of America.
No part of this book may be used or reproduced in any manner whatsoever without written permission except in the case of brief quotations embodied in critical articles and reviews. For information address HarperCollins Children's Books, a division of HarperCollins Publishers, 195 Broadway, New York, NY 10007.
www.harpercollinschildrens.com

ISBN 978-0-06-227827-2

Typography by Catherine San Juan
21 22 23 24 PC/LSCC 10 9 8 7 6 5 4 3 2
❖
First Edition

To everyone harboring their own fire
and to everyone lost in the dark.
May you see the sun again.

the fire never goes out

a memoir in pictures

noelle stevenson

HARPER
An Imprint of HarperCollins*Publishers*

a letter from the author

It is 2009. You are 17 and you are on fire. You have hair that's cut as short as it will go, and it doesn't bother you when people tease you for looking like a lesbian because you know you're not. You wear bows in your hair and bright colors and dresses over jeans. You know a few things very strongly: that you want a boyfriend, that Jesus loves you, that you can hate the sin and love the sinner.

You want the world to see you and hear you, but you don't know yet what you are trying to say.

It is 2011. You are 19 and you are broken. You don't wear the bows or the colors anymore and you hate everything about the you from 2009. You don't know very many things after all, it turns out. You don't have a boyfriend. You don't have Jesus either, and for the first time in your entire life, you're alone inside your mind. And one cold night, a girl crawled into your bed to stay warm, but you're not ready to think too hard about that yet.

You are trying to tell the world who you are, but they don't seem to understand. So you pick up a pen and you draw.

It is 2012. You are 20 and you are going to live forever. The world is infinite and it is all in your favor. You're sleeping on couches and meeting strangers and drinking beers you're not supposed to have yet and kissing boys, and it all comes so easy. You get a tattoo of a star and a boy you like tells you it means you're a lesbian and you laugh about that, but afterward you wear a bracelet over it.

It is 2014 and it is Valentine's Day and you are crying because you know that soon you will no longer have a boyfriend and not only that but you will never have another boyfriend ever again.

It is 2015 and you are 23 and you have been nominated for an award. You are the youngest person to ever be nominated for that award, but you find yourself crying in the bathroom. Everyone has been so kind to you and you don't want to disappoint them. You are tired and you are alone. Now when people call you a lesbian you don't correct them, but the word feels strange in your mouth. It turns out that kissing girls is just as easy as kissing boys, but for some reason you can't kiss her and you don't know why and you can't stop thinking about it.

It is 2016 and you are on fire. You hope you will be the one she kisses at midnight, but when she does, everything changes. You explode like a firework and your heart breaks violently and out of the pieces something beautiful grows. She folds little paper birds for you and you make bread together, and you've never been so happy. The world has never been brighter. The world has never been darker. You wear black to Pride and you cry uncontrollably at the joyful music. You worry that they will end it just as you are beginning.

The next day, you tell the world who you are, and you never look back.

It is 2018 and you are 26 and you are so, so tired. The fire keeps burning, but your insides have turned to ash. There are blisters on your feet and a rattle in your breath, and every night the end of the world plays out in front of your wide-open eyes. You are going to fail. You are going to let everyone down. Your rabbit heart is breaking against your ribs and you are starting to suspect that you will not survive it.

It is 2019 and you are alive.

The cells of your body are dying and growing again every day, and you are always in the process of becoming something new. You're not sure yet who you will be, but you are ready to find out. You know some things a little better now, and your rabbit heart has grown steadier, and you are learning to be gentler to that soft girl with the bow in her hair who is still somewhere inside of you.

This is her story. This is my story.

there is no
HOLY GHOST
inside of me

2011

HAPPY NEW YEAR

DEC 31, 2010

9:00 PM MST

sniff

sniff

hey, honey. How do you feel?
I can't really breathe.

we got you a cake. You can blow out the candles after we watch the game.
ok.

I have no idea what happened to that cake.

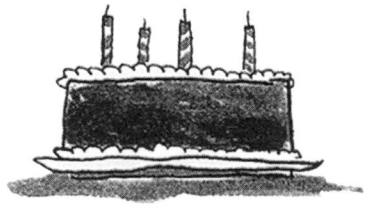

holy ghost

you realize suddenly in the middle of it all

you don't know why but you just go and leave your friends

and you cry once you're outside

because you know you can never go back

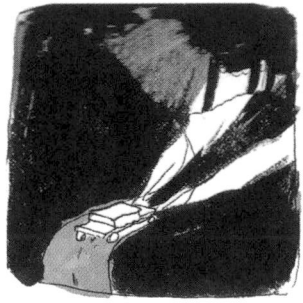

and you drive away until the city lights drop away behind you

you find yourself at the foot of a hill

so you climb

there are some deer nearby

at the top, you just stand

and look at the city lights

the wind blows through the treetops

Who are you?
you say

why won't you ever answer me?

(there's no answer)
(there never is)

so you lie on the grass and look at the sky

you can feel infinity pressing on you from every side

and yet you are alive
and it seems to you that that's a miracle
(even if there's no such thing as miracles)
so you go back
and when you get back
no one notices that you were gone
and no one notices that you're any different
and no one notices
that you'll never be the same.

I haven't had more than 4 consecutive hours of sleep since Saturday

I'm strangely okay though

Before art school, I thought I needed a certain amount of sleep and food

turns out I only need a fraction of that

I'm INVINCIBLE

sophomore year

I have
a demon
inside
of
me

most of
the time
i'm
fine

until

ask me
what's wrong
help me

listen to them
they don't even know
anything's wrong
having fun without me

you could go have
fun with them

just say you're
sorry

let go of your pride

I needed to destroy something
but I didn't want to make a mess

they
were just
scratches
welts

I didn't want
to bleed

they faded
by the end of
the day

I just wanted
an outward
sign that
something was
wrong with
me -
so it wouldn't
be my fault.

people kept dying

not even people
I knew well - kids from high school
but I spent
hours on their
memorial
Facebook pages

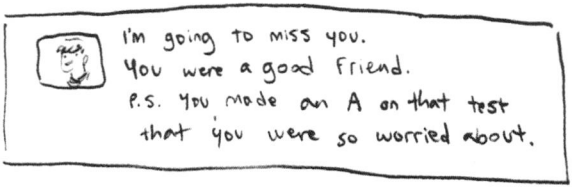

I started walking out
of church.

I couldn't believe
anymore
but the other
option was
unthinkable.

there were good
times too
like the time
we built a fort in the
common area

and we watched
21 Jump street inside

and once
we made a huge
bowl of vegan

cookie
dough
and we
ate all of it
instead of making
cookies

and the
painting of
Edward Cullen
I found at a
thrift store

decorated with
real glitter

and the perfect
fall day where we
went apple picking

"she's dead."

death.

in the end it was the concept of the afterlife that broke me.

But it wasn't my own death that scared me the most.

It all came down to one day in church.

I stayed in there for the rest of the service

I went back one or two more times but I could never quite sit through an entire service again.

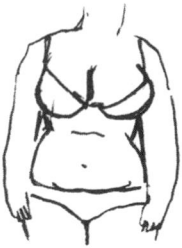

I lost 20 pounds in a semester.

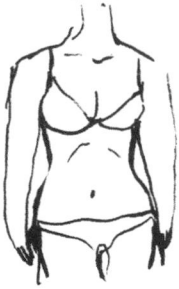

It felt like slowly disappearing

washing away down the drain

I started to have crippling attacks of shaking & sweating

I tried to wake up my roommate the first time but my teeth were chattering too hard to speak the weight loss was my proof that something was wrong, and I needed something to be wrong.

I confided in an older friend that I might be bipolar.

I used to cut my hair as short as I could

I wore colorful layers

bows in my hair and dresses over baggy jeans

but after sophomore year I let my hair get longer

I wore fewer colors and layers and I threw away the bows.

My meltdowns came once a week.

I pushed my friend

I screamed at her when she was just trying to help

this isn't me it can't be

I'm sick it's bipolar it has to be

because
if it's not
then this is
just me
and I am
awful
and mean
and bad

she didn't agree.

but it
didn't matter
in the end
because school
ended and I
went home,
briefly.

the weird thing is,

it never came back.

and I was okay.

for some reason.

I moved out of the dorms. I was going to share the new apartment with one of my old roommates, but she dropped out instead. so I lived alone.

On my own, I could think.

I was empty, but not in a bad way - lighter. freer.

I had lost things.

but maybe

I wouldn't miss them

as much as I thought.

hello
do you
want to date
me check

☐ yes
or

☐ no

(if you check yes
I will look at you
funny and invent
a million reasons
it would never work out)

2011

year in REVIEW

A lot of awesome things happened in my life in 2011! I also drew a lot this year. I was going through my Doodles folder today, and I think it tells the story of my year better than I can. So I decided to compile them into a little backward look at 2011.

In 2011, I took my first Sequential Arts class. It wasn't my first choice, and I almost dropped it. I knew nothing about comics at this point, while my classmates knew all the big names and had been reading comics for years, so I felt kind of behind.

I don't know why I thought this way; I'd actually been drawing comics for years. I was surprised to find that it wasn't actually a super exclusive club, and that there were a lot of different ways to do it.

In 2011, I shaved the side of my head for the first time at a party.

In 2011, I discovered that watching TV while doing homework makes the whole process much more enjoyable. I began watching *Bones*, and started doodling the characters and posting them to Tumblr.

Around this time I started garnering a small following by drawing matadors and lady pirates.

To celebrate, I drew some requests, which opened the gates for fanart. I'd never done much in the way of fanart before, but I was beginning to discover how much fun it was.

In 2011, while watching the Lord of the Rings trilogy for the umpteenth time, I doodled Aragorn, Legolas, and Gimli in modern-day attire, and posted it online.

Within minutes it had over 600 notes, and after drawing the rest of the Fellowship in the same vein I gained nearly a thousand followers in one night. And thus, the Broship of the Ring was born.

I ended up watching the Lord of the Rings trilogy more times this year than any one person should.

In 2011, I got an apartment in Baltimore and lived by myself for a while... with a ball python as a roommate.

I was working two jobs, one of which was an eight-hour night shift. Eight hours of wakefulness five times a week gave me plenty of time to doodle and catch up on TV series.

I drew myself with a hole in the middle a lot. My life was changing, and although I was happy, I couldn't help but feel that I had lost something in a way I couldn't quite verbalize.

I also didn't wear pants very often. (It was hot.)

In 2011, my friend Aimee and I attended the midnight showing of X-Men: First Class. We were drawing fanart almost before we were out of the theater.

I did a couple of quick, loose panel comics about Mystique getting in the way of everything, which set the mold for future Tumblr comics.

It was a good summer for superhero movies. *Thor* and *Captain America* got me deeply invested in Marvel characters and excited for *The Avengers*!

In 2011, I had a short sort-of internship in Washington, DC. I wore a blouse and fought my way through DC traffic a couple of times a week. I was also paying my own rent for the first time, and I felt like a proper adult.

I moved into another apartment before school started. My would-be roommate ended up not coming back, meaning I was living alone again, and I wasn't sure I wanted to. It turned out to be okay, though, as things often do.

In 2011, I survived both an earthquake and a hurricane, both of which proved to be pretty anticlimactic.

what happened

what it felt like

In fall 2011, I was taking 18 credits and classes with Sam Bosma and Kali Ciesemier, meaning that fall 2011 was a semester of very little sleep, not enough of the right kinds of food, and a lot of long Netflix-and-coffee-fueled homework jams.

Weirdly enough, though, I was kind of having a blast. I was the most comfortable with myself that I'd ever been, and without even realizing it, that hole in my middle seemed to be gone.

In short, 2011 was a good year.

be still.

2012

I'm fine
just understand

you'll be okay
but you'll lose some things

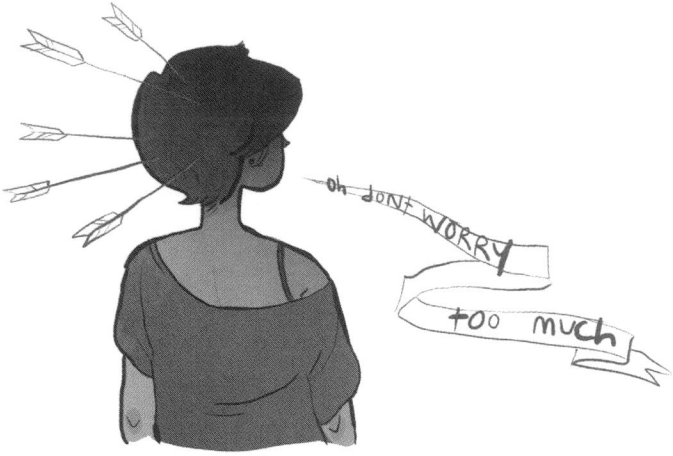
oh dont worry
too much

this is what
you wanted

I was talking to my brother about women's attitudes toward their bodies, especially regarding weight/fat, and when he said "most guys don't notice/care about that kind of thing," I tried to explain why it was a lot more complicated than that. I ended up telling this story.

Body image is something that's so hard to talk about, and it's hard to express body positivity without sounding cheesy, false, or overly simplistic. But I'm gonna try. This is only my own experience, and it didn't magically cure me of all my body image issues—but it was a major turning point for me nonetheless.

Those bodies were my only reference for whether or not my own body was acceptable.

she doesn't look like the Victoria's secret models. She has so much body hair she's got flab and creases and dimples.

...why didn't anyone tell me those things were beautiful?

But now, no one had to tell me. I could see.

we drew a lot of models.

None of them looked anything like a Victoria's secret model - they didn't look like me either, or like each other. why should they try?

I'd always been told we were all beautiful just the way we are. I never believed it.

Until now.

all those bodies fit together in infinitely fascinating ways, and the stuff I hated before - thighs and bellies and wrinkles and bulges - now they were the best part.

I used to dream about a little boy in striped pajamas
I had to save him in every dream
from snakes
tornadoes
floods
until one night I couldn't save him
I know who he was
he was my brother
who was never born
I never saw him in a dream again

hey
it's ok

you can do this
get up

we're an adult now
and there's work to be done

sometimes I think I would like to have
ABS
yeeeah
but I don't care enough to actually work out or anything
eh, whatever

this is how you get abs right

you don't even remember what it's like to want love anymore
you can't even see the appeal

did your heart really break that much last time?

and why did it never grow back?

yes I'm fine
I'm fine

Dishes

year in REVIEW

If you've been following me since the Broship of the Ring in 2011, you know how far I've come in just a little over a year. This blog and the doodles that I post on it end up serving as a scrapbook or diary—so for the second time, I thought I'd compile them into a comprehensive look back at my life in 2012.

Wow, a lot happened in 2012. It was a GOOD YEAR.

In 2012, I signed up for an Advanced Sequential Art class with Joan Hilty. By this point, I was PRETTY sure I dug comics, but this was going to be the final test. I hadn't made a comic longer than four pages, and it had always been an ordeal. I wanted to see if I was really capable of sustaining a longer story in comic form. And I was pretty sure what the project was I wanted to tackle—I wanted to continue Nimona's story.

I'd already done two NIMONA pages in 2011 for another class—over the course of the semester in Advanced Sequential I cranked out sixteen more. Joan was an incredibly supportive teacher with great advice. I streamlined my comic-making process, and realized that yes, I was a comics person forevermore. I could visualize Nimona's story so clearly that I made a resolution: I would make NIMONA a real webcomic and I would finish it.

In 2012, I saw the *Hunger Games*, made some dumb comics, and got a buttload of attention for it.

In 2012, I started looking for an internship for the summer. I had no idea where to start, so I took my quest to Tumblr, hoping that I had some followers who could hook me up with a lead. That's how I got in touch with Shannon Watters, editor at BOOM! Studios, who was looking for an intern...and before long I was making plans to fly across the country and spend the summer in LA.

In 2012, I was getting SOOOPER pumped about the Avengers. Due in no small part to the Avengers cartoon Earth's Mightiest Heroes, I formed a deep fondness for the Hulk and Hawkeye and drew a lot of fanart of them.

My Avengers fanart attracted the attention of Gallery1988, who invited me to send some art to their Avengers-themed gallery show...a show that was attended by Joss Whedon himself.

I made myself a Hawkeye costume for the midnight showing and I was the only one in the whole theater in costume.

I drew about ten billion Avengers comics and garnered a fair bit of attention for that, too. It ended up bringing Charlie Olsen, a literary agent at Inkwell Management, to my blog—but we'll get to that in a bit.

In 2012, my piece was accepted into the Society of Illustrators student scholarship show!

In 2012, I drew some Pokeymans.

In 2012, I was desperately searching for a place to stay in LA for the summer. It was harder than I had anticipated.

I thought I found a place, and then, the day before I was to get on the plane, it fell through. Luckily, my dad had a friend who lived in Santa Monica, and they very graciously let me sleep on their couch in their entertainment room for two weeks until I could find another place. They were very nice to me and I had a great time hanging out with their two young daughters, but frankly Santa Monica TERRIFIED me.

Fortunately, I found a room to rent in Mid-City, a much less "bougie" part of town, and felt much more at home there. I lived with two USC med students and barely saw them at all.

My internship at BOOM! was going GREAT. They were such a laid-back group of people and I got to look at comics all day, and I loved it.

LA was VERY kind to me. I got lots of messages from internet strangers inviting me places, and I'm not sure all of them really expected me to say yes but I was pretty desperate for friends and I ended up meeting loads of new people and EVERY SINGLE ONE OF THEM WAS GREAT. What are the odds of that? From a movie at the ArcLight with Anita Sarkeesian to a Drink-and-Draw at Pen Ward's house, to watching Jurassic Park in a cemetery, to a Bad Robot Fourth of July party, to brunch at the cool hipster joints and comedy shows at Meltdown, I was having a blast and being shown around LA by all the cool Angelenos.

In 2012, I was on my first panel at ALA! We talked about fanart. I attended my VERY FIRST San Diego Comic-Con! It was kind of my first con in general. It was amazing. It blew my mind. I met Michael Emerson.

I was working the BOOM! booth as an intern, but I still had TONS of people come up to say hi, get autographs, and have pictures taken with me. And I got to track down and fangirl over some of my own favorite artists! It was a generally awesome and overwhelming experience.

In 2012, I launched NIMONA as a webcomic, with the help of the great Stephen Warren. It was great. And scary.

As I mentioned before, Charlie Olsen found his way to my blog through my Avengers comics, and found his way to my webcomic through my blog. He contacted me shortly after with the interest of representing me and helping me to get NIMONA in front of some publishers.

In short, summer 2012 was incredible. I'd never lived in such a big city before, with so much happening all the time. Everything that I could have hoped would come out of that summer, did. So it was sad when, at the end of the summer, it was time to go home. The thought of going back to Baltimore and finishing my last year of school was a bit depressing, to be honest. And it really did feel like I was putting down roots in LA. This was everything that art school had prepared me for, after all. But in the end, I did go back.

every day it was sunny and cloudless.

I took my parents up to New York to meet with Charlie and decide whether or not to sign with him. Feeling pretty good about it, I signed with Inkwell Management shortly after that, and moved back to Baltimore for my last year of school.

Unfortunately, my parents' business was going through some rough times, and their credit suffered. As a result, I was denied my parent plus loan, which was nearly $20,000. I was worried for a while that I wouldn't be going back to school after all–fortunately the school came through for me and scraped up some scholarships, and we made ends meet in the end–with the help of everyone who bought prints from my shop and donated to my comic!!

In 2012, while I was in school, Charlie was shopping me around to publishers in New York—and we ended up striking a deal with HarperCollins. Through a completely unlikely series of circumstances, a chain of events that started in 2011 with a dumb kid and a blog, I had a book deal.

In 2012, I turned 21 at last. In the past few months, I've illustrated the cover to Ryan North's Choose-Your-Own-Adventure Hamlet book, which set the record as Kickstarter's most-funded publishing project, AND Rainbow Rowell's YA novel Fangirl with St. Martin's Press. On January 2nd, you'll be able to buy my very first published short comic, a four-page backup comic in Fionna and Cake #1, from BOOM! Studios! It's almost like I'm a real grown-up person.

It's been an incredible journey, you guys. Thank you so much for supporting me all this way. I couldn't have done it without you <3

2013

First day of weights class

the next morning

laundry

#1:
get nakers or hair will get in your bra and that is the worst
thinning shears... good for hair? who knows!
clippers also

#2:
hack away at bits that are poofy

#3:
it is your worst haircut ever.
There's hair everywhere and it still somehow gets in your bra.

Holy
Week

you see yourself as pretty harmless, mostly

and a thick black slime rushes out and covers your body and it transforms you

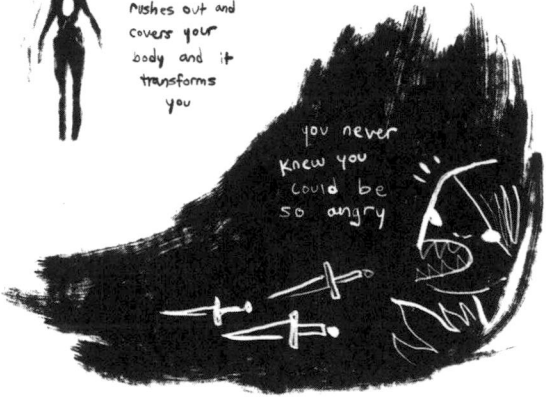

but then it flows away as quick as it came

and it's just you left there

and you see what you've done

that wasn't me
that was the monster that lives inside me

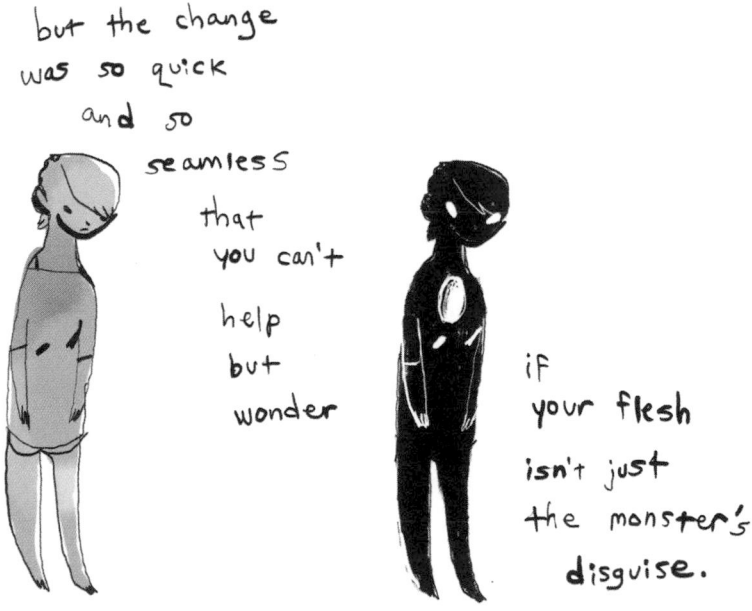
but the change was so quick and so seamless that you can't help but wonder
if your flesh isn't just the monster's disguise.

I am afraid

of money
of death
of how my hands
shake all the time

of burning out
of going up in flames

of there being nothing real inside me
and that one day everyone will
be able to see that

2013

year in REVIEW

For the past two years, I've been compiling year-in-review posts on New Year's Eve.

2011 was the year everything started happening.

In 2012, things continued to happen.

So you will be pleased to know that in 2013, things happened even more.

In 2013, I was working on my last semester of art school. I had become disenchanted with the environment—I was tired of being told what to do and wanted to focus my full attention on my own projects. After the summer I spent in Los Angeles in 2012, I'd felt my life beginning, only to put it on hold for another year to earn what felt like a largely pointless document.

It was always my plan to go back to LA as soon as I finished school, but I knew it was a hard sell. It was on the other side of the country, expensive, and I didn't have a specific reason that I needed to be there, like a job. So when my parents came up to Baltimore for a visit, I ran the idea past them, not expecting an enthusiastic response. To my surprise, my mom calmly and practically told me I needed a plan for how to get there, and helped me figure out some options. Before I knew it, it had become real. I had a plan.

I buckled down for my last semester of senior year, but due to a generous share of senioritis, it wasn't always easy...

I enjoyed the time I spent with my friends senior year, but still, I was ready to go.

All of my mixed feelings toward my school culminated on graduation day, when they called me by the wrong name.

It felt like a cruel kick out of the door. I was going to be in debt for what seemed like the rest of my life to pay back nearly 100K in student loan debts in order to have attended school here, and they didn't even know my name.

But it didn't matter. I was done, I was gone, I had earned that piece of paper—fortunately with my name spelled right on it. And looking back now that I have some distance, I can see what that school did for me, and how I wouldn't be where I am now without it. My time at art school was filled with extreme highs and lows, but it's where I became an adult.

I had a ticket to fly to LA only a week after graduation. I couldn't bring much with me—only what I could fit in two suitcases. I was starting to get nervous—California was so far away! What if it wasn't like how I remembered it?

But as soon as I stepped out of LAX, I was reassured. It had always felt like a place that I belonged. It was big, exciting, and full of possibilities.

I moved into my new apartment and met my roommate and her two dogs. I bought a car and a bunch of IKEA furniture, and before too long I had begun my new life in LA. I was paying my rent, bills, and car payments by myself. I was making a living off of my art in one of the most exciting cities I'd ever been in—living the dream!

In 2013, I signed with a talent agency in LA, the Agency for the Performing Arts, who specialized in TV and movies. They sent me out for general meetings with all kinds of neat TV and animation studios, which was super exciting!

I went to San Diego Comic-Con with BOOM! Studios for the second time. Despite my body sabotaging me with various illnesses, I had an awesome, if overwhelming, great time.

The summer passed and fall began and for the first time I didn't have to go back to school. It was awesome. I had friends, opportunities, and there was always something cool to do.

Although when it came to dating and relationships, I was in no better shape than ever. It seemed that when it came to romance, my life had been a series of bad timing and being on various sides of unreciprocated interest.

But then, unexpectedly, that changed, and I was amazed to find that maybe sometimes your orbit can line up with another person's just right.

Natasha!
can I help?

oh no! Natasha!

NATASHAAAAA

In 2013, my art graced the covers of not one but TWO books, as well as an audiobook and a couple of comics.

In 2013, I wrote an episode of Bravest Warriors, which will air soon!
And I worked with What Pumpkin on Namco High.
And of course, drew some pretty badass moments in my webcomic NIMONA!

...and that's not to mention several secret projects I can't talk about just yet!

In 2013, I won the Slate Cartoonist Studio Prize for Best Webcomic, was nominated for a Harvey Award, and Paste named me one of the top ten comic artists as well as the best webcomic of 2013!

In 2013, I attended comic conventions in New York City, Baltimore, Bethesda, Washington DC, Seattle, San Diego, and Los Angeles, to name just a few!
And finally, in 2013, I turned 22!

2013 was good to me. I'm exactly where I want to be, and I'm so lucky to be supporting myself by telling stories, just like I've always wanted. I'm so excited for 2014–there's still so much to be done!

2014

I am
on fire

literally on fire
all the
time

aaaaahhh

oh my god oh my god oh my god

are you
ready,
baby?

At the airport

i dont love
anyone

zzzz

year in REVIEW

In 2014, I:

- finished my first webcomic
- got a job writing for cartoons
- had a breakup
- went to a con that turned into a meme
- got a dog!!
- saw some pretty bad movies
- wrote some comics
- worked hard
- grew a lot

2015 is gonna be a big one—in just a few short months my first graphic novel, NIMONA, will hit the shelves! The first *Lumberjanes* trade will also drop, and you'll get to see my first work for Marvel and DC, along with some other exciting announcements.

I still have so much to learn and so far to grow. Thanks for taking this journey with me, and I hope this new year is a good one for you all <3

2015

is this
what
you
wanted
to be?

Clouds

to hold them
soft as cotton candy
lighter than air

to
sleep on
them

to run
across
them –
to explore their caves and
mountains.

but you find
out, soon enough,
that you can't touch
clouds. They're nothing
but condensation, cold
and wet, and not
fluffy at all.

this is what my love for you
is like.

you are nice to see
from my airplane window
but I am safe here.

I can't touch you.
and if I tried, there'd be nothing
there - just coldness, wetness,
a sickening drop.

I know you'll never love me.
That's okay.
That's why I chose you.

I only wanted the desire
and none of the risk.

but there's always a part of me that doesn't understand.

doesn't know this isn't real.

and I dream of flying.

you forget it isn't real.

you'll never fly like that.

and the clouds are only water.

CAMP

year in REVIEW

Is 2015 already over?! How did that happen?

2015 has been the goal year for me for a while. It was the culmination of several years of hard work and rapid climbing, so to see it come to fruition was...well, frankly, terrifying. And amazing, of course. And heartbreaking. And exhilarating.

In 2015, the school project turned webcomic turned graphic novel that I spent more than three years working on was finally published by HarperCollins. It became a real book you can hold in your hands and buy in a store. It premiered on the *New York Times* bestseller list.

In 2015, the first trade of *Lumberjanes* was published as well. It, too, premiered on the *New York Times* bestseller list.

In 2015, my first published work for both Marvel and DC hit stands: a story in the *Thor Annual* that I wrote, and a Wonder Woman story that I illustrated. A few months later, my first miniseries for Marvel premiered, a weird little YA high school story set in the middle of the massive summer event Secret Wars, carrying on the title of *Runaways*.

In 2015, my first TV writer credit hit the air with the premiere of season 2 of *Wander Over Yonder*.

In 2015, *Lumberjanes* won two Eisners and a Harvey.

In 2015, NIMONA made the shortlist of five books to be nominated for a National Book Award in children's literature. I was only the 3rd person to be shortlisted for a graphic novel and the youngest ever nominee.

In 2015, both NIMONA and *Lumberjanes* went on to be optioned as movies.

2015 was a banner year. And 2015 was one of the hardest, scariest years of my life.

I'd climbed higher and faster than I ever thought was possible, and suddenly I was terrified of falling. I couldn't stop looking down. Ever since art school, I was afraid of burnout. Burnout was final. Burnout was a death sentence. And in 2015, I officially burned out.

But, well, I got better?

In 2015, I stepped down from a project that was and remains very dear to me...and was one of the most exhausting, emotionally draining projects I've ever worked on. The choice to depart was entirely mine, and it was entirely the right thing to do. I needed to get better, and that meant certain things needed to be left behind.

I think it's time
that you shed your skin
and climb out of the hole you have dug yourself in

here's your second chance.
what will you do?

In 2015, I moved out of the apartment where I lived alone and moved into a house in a quiet neighborhood with a roommate. And thus began the era of Galhalla.

Galhalla became a place of healing, of gathering, of commiseration and support, of lights and music and movie nights and way too much take-out Indian food. It became a safe place, a place to take pride in. It represented a fresh start to me.

I thought I'd been strong before, but I'd been isolated and closed off. I thought being strong meant being as hard as diamonds and never letting anyone get close enough to hurt me. And to be sure, my faith in others was shaken a lot in 2015.

you grew up, but not really.

you fell in love so fast.

that was the last of your childish loves

before your soft baby heart crystallized

you moved on and you were fine.

you were hard as diamonds.

and before too long you discovered what it was like to be on the other side

they liked your sharp, hard, shiny crystals.

so did you.

you thought
maybe if you
acted it
out

you would feel the
fire again

but you never
did

did you actually
want to?

why are you doing
this anyway?

your heart
doesn't feel
broken. you
just feel
guilty.

the
truth is, you don't
mind being
alone.

you're not a little girl
anymore.

you don't want
the things you
thought you
wanted then.

you're fine.

you're hard as diamonds.

But that's not what strength is. The ability to adapt and grow, to let yourself rest, to ask for help when you need it...that's real strength. And I grew so much in 2015. I feel every day that I'm becoming more and more the person I was always meant to be. I've learned to identify the things that are most important to me and focus on those things, and I've learned to let go of the things that just don't make the cut.

There's no way 2016 will be as flashy as 2015 was, but that's fine with me. I'm ready to put my head down and get back to work. There are so many things I still want to do and I'm nowhere near done. I'm stronger, I'm calmer, and I've learned a lot. There are still so many stories to tell.

I'm still afraid, but it doesn't stop my heart anymore. Occasionally, I sleep through the night. And I have a lot of great people by my side to help me. I'm learning to put away the diamond exterior and let people get close again. To be good up close instead of just from a distance. I'm letting myself be happy.

So here's to you, 2015. Thanks for giving me so many great things and for kicking my ass in the process.

I'm 24 today. So bring on 2016. Let's make some stories!

2016

they say that
red birthmarks show how
you were killed in a
past life

I have a
small one

just over
my heart

I wonder how
it happened

Track 1
Riptide (the Taylor Swift cover)

you were bold, & young, &
drunk on loneliness.

you were pretty good
at kissing girls

and pretty good at waking
up alone.

you didn't mind.

your cruel young heart liked the taste of
blood, & it was better for it to go hungry.

but you never saw her coming.

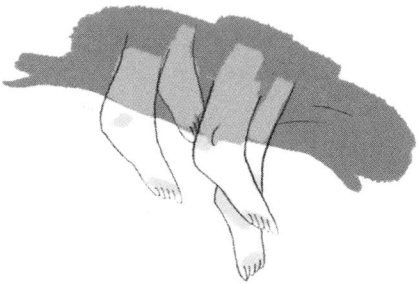

you crashed
into
each
other

so
slowly

and
so hard.

In the morning, she was still there.

your cold young heart was afraid
and you ran.

Track 2
Do I wanna know? - Arctic Monkeys

there were cracks in your
hard baby heart.

you couldn't stay away.

Oh, you knew it was a bad idea.

but it kept happening.

you never slept at all those nights. You didn't want to miss anything.

and what do you do with a shooting star?

you make a wish.

oh baby, you're in too deep.

Track 3 -

Don't Go - Allison Weiss

she left
a toothbrush
at your place.

~~it gave you hope.~~

you tried not to hope.

~~you wished she could just stay for coffee.~~

you knew better
than to wish.

~~you wanted her to just be with you.~~

no.

you knew how this worked.

Track 4 -
Keep you on my side - Chvrches

stay.

I can't do this anymore
✓ sent

Track 5 -
Friday I'm in Love - The Cure

...
how are you doing?
delivered
it's Friday.
I'm in love.

Track 6 -

Wait For Me - Allison Weiss

you never were good at staying away from each other.

you helped her pick things out for her new apartment

what if -

not yet.

Track 7

wherever is your Heart - Brandi Carlile

you made me feel like
I was always falling

always falling down
without a place to land

somewhere in the distance
heard you calling

oh it hurt so bad
to let go
of your
hand

wherever is your heart

I call home

year in REVIEW

You know, I almost didn't think I was going to do one of these this year! After a year of quietly working away on various secret projects, it felt like I didn't have a lot to show. And the world after November 8th feels like waking up from a hopeful dream to realize that everything's been fucked for a long, long time, and it's likely to get worse. So how could 2016 have been a good year? But to be honest... 2016, while complicated, was one of the happiest years I've ever had.

Literally the first thing I did in 2016 was fall in love with someone I shouldn't have. Still, as someone historically terrible at being in love, it was easy to push aside any misgivings and self-preservation instincts I might have and just fall, hard.

I'd always had an idea of myself as a very emotionally tough person who was at best incredibly skeptical of romance. I liked being single, and I was good at it.

I was
as hard as diamonds.

bright & beautiful
and untouchable.

I wasn't always like that.

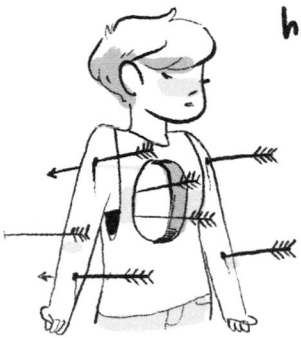

how strange
to have such pride
in the part
of myself that
seemed to be
missing

But something had started to change in me. After throwing myself entirely into my work for several years and seeing it pay off in a big way in 2015, I was tired. And I was scared. And it was hard to see exactly what I was working toward when it seemed like I risked going up in flames when I'd only just begun.

the fire never goes out

sometimes it keeps you warm

sometimes it makes your blood run cold

It turned out I wanted more. I loved my work, but I wanted something that could love me back.

I started losing a lot of sleep—partially from stress, and partially because what had started as an uncomplicated crush was quickly spiraling out of control.

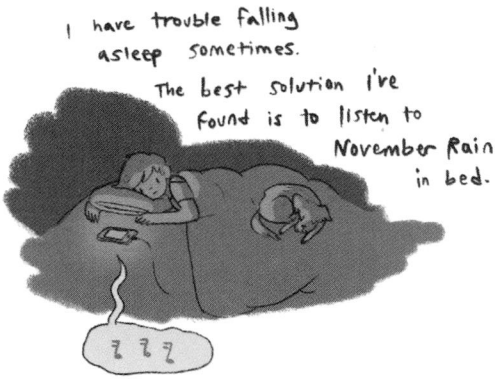

January seemed to last a million years. Nothing that happened next was pretty.

For all
the walls
I thought I
had
not a single one held.

perhaps they'd never
been so strong.

go to sleep

you didn't do anything wrong.

you didn't.

right?

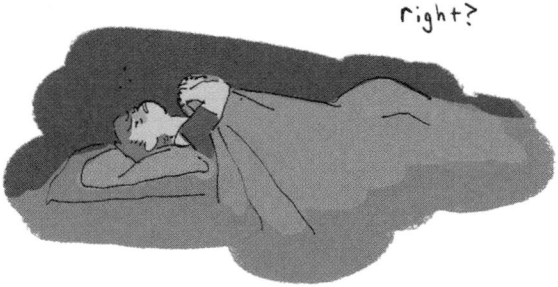

just

go to sleep.

And then, it was over.

your bed isn't growing any colder

or any more empty.

your broken heart

still beats.

Except it wasn't. Because we just weren't smart enough to let it be.

but in my softness
I was as strong as I'd
ever been.

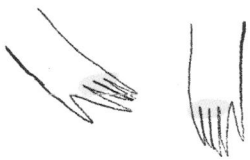

and I
reached

again

for your hand.

January was finally over, and suddenly I wasn't alone anymore. And cautiously, we made our way forward.

Simple things

- a root beer float

- a toothbrush

- a tiny dog trying to walk in the tall grass

- the sound of waves

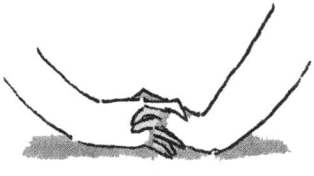

I'd like it if you stayed

in schools
in theaters
in churches
in the streets

I think it has probably
always felt like
this.

It had always felt like I'd inherited a good world, a world that had no choice but to keep getting better, and I would surely benefit. As the year wore on, that illusion was shattered again and again.

So here we are. 2016 is over, and no one knows what's going to happen next. It may be that 2016 is the best year I'll see for a while, but I'm not giving up, and I'm not alone.

Thanks, everyone, for coming with me this far. It's time to wake up and it's time to fight. I hope we'll all be okay in the end, but I won't leave it at hope anymore. I'm grateful for the good things I have, and whatever 2017 has in store, I'll try to be ready.

2017

try to be
calm

your fear of doing wrong
is keeping you from
doing good.

this is what
you wanted

ain't
you proud?

you're
not
evil

you are a
mundane, selfish
kind of bad
and that is
what you're always
feared, isn't it?

you do kind things
for praise

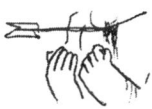

or to feel
better

you fear hurting people

but maybe because you
fear being disliked.

you're not strong
or brave
in the way you
want to be

you wanted
to be seen

to be loved

it only
made you more
lonely.

you are
a goat among sheep

weeds among wheat

a vessel destined
for destruction

It's what they
always said you were.

oh child, they'll
never love you.

I like girly shit but I'm not very girly
I like manly shit but im not very manly
usually it doesn't bother me but sometimes it does

honestly I don't want to wear a suit
It's just better than a dress
I want to be beautiful but I don't know how

I have
so many
good things

they are
what I always
wanted

so I
cannot admit
that they are
destroying me

I want to
be stronger
than this

but
I don't think
I have it as bad
as most

I have always
been able to
stand up again

Easter 2017

happy Easter! How are you?
I'm good!
how is Molly?
?!
She's good!
does grandma know Molly is my girlfriend?
...
iMessage
yeah she's not that naive!
...
I've never been good at having secrets

I feel like I'm going crazy when I have to keep something inside

but sometimes it is the unselfish way

I think she figured it out after that picture of y'all at Pride

She took it really well

before my opa died he asked me

I didn't know what he meant.

He didn't even remember my name at the time.

but I said

It's nice to not have a secret anymore

year in REVIEW

you're going to pay off your student loans! All of them!!
oh also you're gay
super gay
hey
it's okay
I know you still need to date boys right now, and those feelings are real.
eventually it's gonna start to make sense, though. take your time. you'll get there.

...Are we happy?
...
you know this is what you want to be doing.
you love it.
but?
but it hurts too.
I mean
all that before you're 26. How could you not be afraid of what comes next?
you don't want to disappoint anyone, but you will. You'll break in big and small ways, and you'll never be the same.
and guilty. You'll feel guilty a lot.

I miss being you sometimes.
Me? I'm a mess. I'm hungry and lonely and cold all the time because the radiator doesn't work and I'm scared of the landlord. And I never sleep.
Yeah. I guess you'll miss that one day.
You'll miss when the world could be anything, and anywhere is better than here.

I'm proud of you. I know you've waited so long to hear someone say it. You fought your way out of the dark.
I will too.

It never does go away, does it?
No. I don't think so.
I know you don't like to think about me. you don't want to hope for something and be disappointed.
you know what you want to do, but not who you want to be.
But soon, you'll be me and you'll have to figure it out.

there's a lot of work to do still.
but it's okay. we got this.

2018

Love letter to a D&D character

My first D&D character was a pretty typical first D&D character: a chaotic evil teen tiefling warlock

She gave me the chance the explore melodramatic, messy, angry feelings I'd always felt but had no outlet for

So in our new campaign, I chose a new kind of character: Quorrin, middle-aged halfling sorcerer. She was a washed-up former child star & recent divorcee looking for a fresh start.

but
no sooner
had she
embarked on
her new career,
than she and her new companions
were cursed by a demon
that would eventually
destroy them

Still, she
didn't let it get her
down. Determined to
"say yes to life,"
Quorrin did
her best to
take care of
the group,
electing herself
"the mom"
despite being
vastly unqualified

Quorrin embodied both the traits I envied and the traits I feared.
what is it like to rebuild your life after so many disappointments, even when you're afraid?

Knowing it was probably her last journey Quorrin threw herself into adventures like she'd never had before

In the end,
Quorrin was
ready to die
especially
if it
would save
her friends.
as the curse took hold,
knowing that the
world would only ever
remember them as monsters,
the former child
star who had once
dreamed of one day
playing the tragic
female lead
devoted herself to
keeping a careful
record of their stories.

but in the end, what she had to learn to do was live...
and this time, really say yes to life.

Evolution

I don't think this is right
this is what the dudes wear!
ur terrible son Cody
wat
queer eye for the depressed lesbian
take care of urself bitch

year in REVIEW

It's been a big year with several big triumphs. The show I've been working on for three years finally premiered, and I got engaged to the best girl in the world. I've never felt more lucky, proud, and loved...but I had another, more personal and harder won victory this year, and I'd like to talk about that first.

This is about mental health, and it's long. Minor trigger warning for things related to that.

I do these posts every year, and have since 2011. Some years, including last year, I wasn't sure if I should continue doing them. The posts encouraged a narrative that I disagreed with as much as I desperately sought to live up to it: that my accomplishments and my youth gave me value, that I was always on the upward climb, that burnout was an easily resolved footnote, that I was young and sharp and fine, I was fine and I would always be fine.

It was as shortsighted as it was unsustainable. The truth was, something was wrong and had been wrong for a long time.

At the start of the year, and when I made last year's comic, I was already close to hitting the wall. I had thrown myself into work, and the show, and I was losing myself in it. I wasn't sleeping. I no longer felt any connection to my own body.

I was doing everything right, I thought: I was working out, going to therapy, taking breaks, I had an incredibly kind and patient partner who was always there for me. I didn't understand why I couldn't just, through force of will, make myself okay.

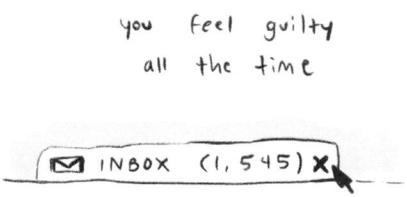

I was burning through energy stores that I didn't have, and I knew it but I couldn't stop. There was something in me that wouldn't let me. I identified it commonly in my drawings as a fire. I'd felt it for years, at varying levels of intensity, but now it seemed that it was burning out of control and it was going to take me with it.

It made me feel like I was living my life in a perpetual state of fight-or-flight–usually fight. At first, my fierce and stubborn temperament was a benefit in the environment I was in. It was clear to me that showing weakness, even for a moment, would be the end. But it was hard to know when to stop fighting, and fighting takes its toll.

you are not
strong

just stubborn.

your
scales are
sharp.

your fire
burns hot.

you can inflict
hurt without
even trying.

but
you are fragile.

your bones break
so easily and
they never
quite heal.

who will care
for you when
your fire turns
to ash?

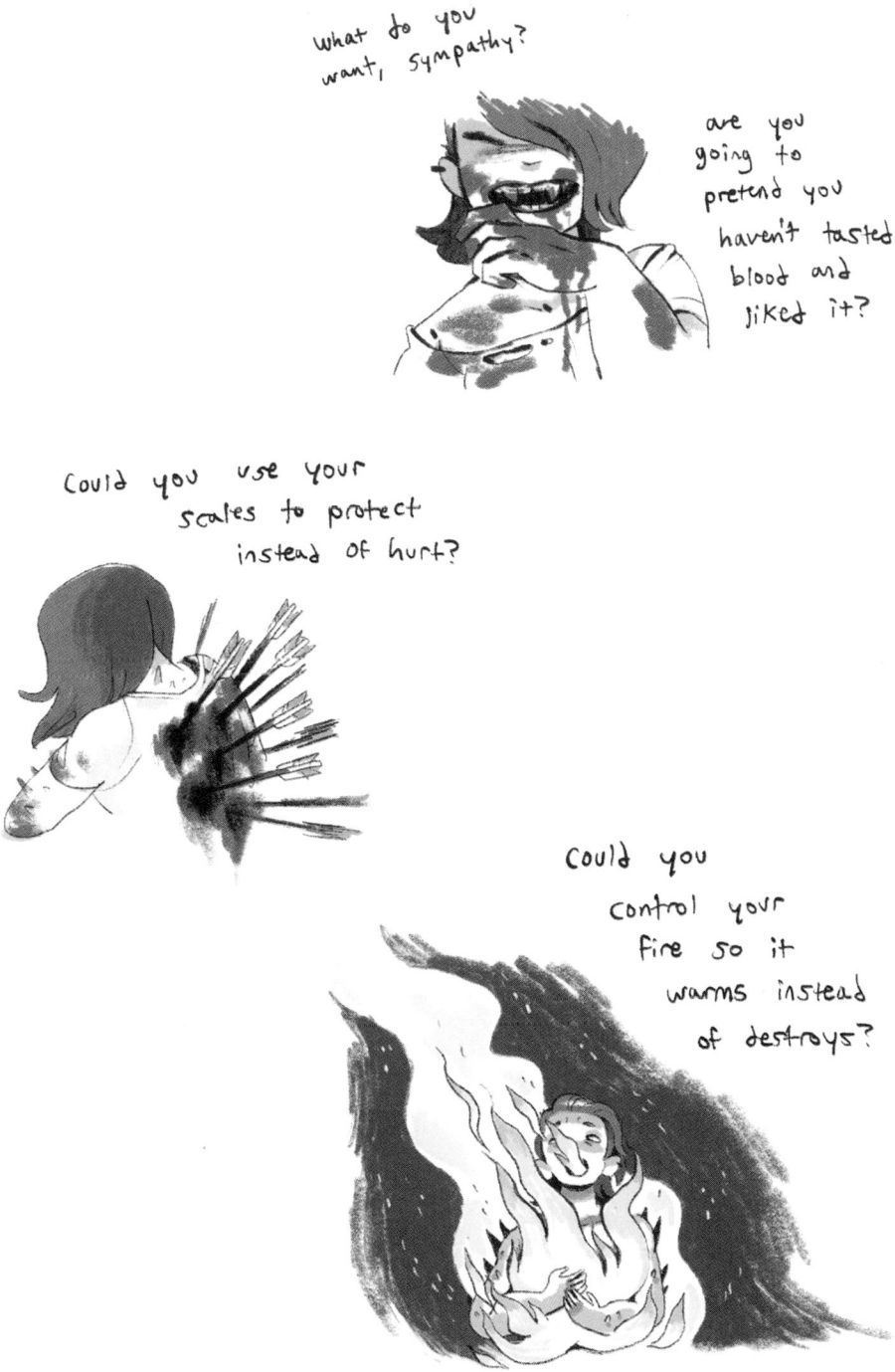
What do you want, sympathy?
are you going to pretend you haven't tasted blood and liked it?
Could you use your scales to protect instead of hurt?
Could you control your fire so it warms instead of destroys?

The show was everything to me, and it was hard to see beyond it. I was keenly aware of how lucky I was to be a showrunner, but I also took the success of the show and the well-being of the crew incredibly personally, and so the guilt of *letting everyone down* convinced me that I was not allowed to be happy in the role—that it would be irresponsible.

you let the wolves have it, but it's okay.

Each bite you feel a little less.

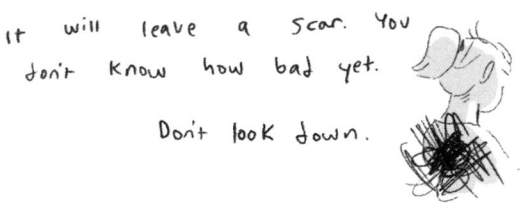

You can do it.
You are sturdy.

You will be everything to everyone.
You will make it to the end.

Then maybe you will get your body back.

and maybe, when it heals, it will be beautiful.

I was so tired, but the fire was still there, and it propelled me stubbornly forward even as it consumed everything inside of me. I thought I could fix everything if I just tried harder...and if I didn't fix things, no one would. I lived in constant dread of the one small slip or mistake that would ruin everything forever. I carried it all, in obsessive detail, in my head, and eventually I stopped being able to turn it off.

Admitting that something was wrong would mean that there was something wrong with me—that I hadn't done a good job, that I wasn't cut out for this, that I had failed. So despite all the red flags, I just kept pushing through.

And my body started to fail.

I think I am destroying myself

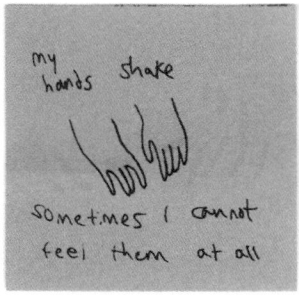
my hands shake
sometimes I cannot feel them at all

uhh
I forget to breathe
or I cannot breathe at all

I can't stay awake

I can't stay asleep

sometimes I can only see the edges of my eyes

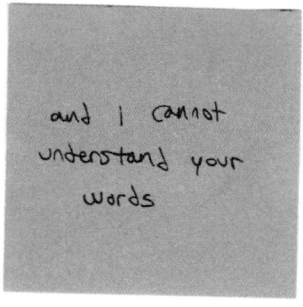
and I cannot understand your words

I don't know how to fix it

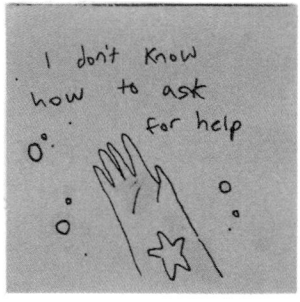
I don't know how to ask for help

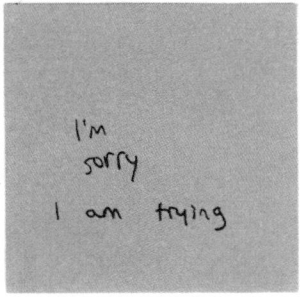
I'm sorry
I am trying

this is not how I wanted to be

For so long I'd put all my personal value in my success, as much as I knew that I shouldn't. I had climbed so high, never really stopping to rest, and I was so scared of falling—I didn't think I'd survive it.

I didn't know that falling was exactly what I needed.

here's
what
they
don't tell you about
climbing
mountains

almost
everyone who dies
dies on the
way down.

the summit,
as much as
you want
it,

is only the
halfway
point.

and night
will be here soon,

and there will be no way
to go but down,

and you will
be so tired.

will you
fall in
plain sight,

a monument
to those
who come
after
you?

will you
vanish into
the darkest depths,
never to
be seen
again?

I won't get into exactly what happened—maybe another time. But it was brutal, and swift, and merciless. This was it, the thing I'd been most afraid of. I was going to be assigned the label of "difficult woman," another one who *just couldn't take the pressure*.

My self-image shattered. But the truth was, there hadn't been much left of it to begin with.

And finally I knew what I had to do.

There's something strangely calming about the fire outside becoming hotter than the one inside. I got back up, put on nice clothes, and stood my ground.

It turns out there can be freedom in the falling, and strength in the breaking.

And finally...I sought out help.

you're not okay,
but you will be.

you are not
done fighting
yet

& you will see
the sun
again.

I saw a psychiatrist and finally got a diagnosis I'd needed for a long time.

Everything fell into place.

The diagnosis alone was a huge relief. It offered context for my racing mind, twitching fingers, the long sleepless nights, the pervasive dread and surging panic, the darkest hopeless lows and vibrating burning highs. I wasn't just falling apart. This was something I could face, and manage.

it's
been a
hard
few months

I've been
sad for a
very long
time

I thought
some people
must burn very
hot

for a very
short time.

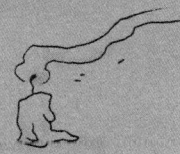

I am
not so
sad now.

the fire has a
name

and
it no longer
consumes me

and I am
stronger than I
ever
knew.

I went on medication.

I had always been afraid of medication. It was easy to romanticize the fire in my brain, and internalize the pervasive notion that it was what made me strong, interesting, creative, and that medication would take that away. It took being pushed to my breaking point to realize that it wasn't worth it.

It would have been worth it anyway, but being on medication has in no way lessened my capacity for feeling or creating. It's made creating easier—it's made my feelings stronger and more sure because I know that they're real. I can see myself again. The face in the mirror is mine. I know what I want, and what I need, and I trust myself for the first time in a long time. The joy of creating has come back.

It was not the diagnosis or the medication alone that helped me get better. I was carried through the darkest parts by the strength of those around me—my awesome and powerful coworkers, the women who kindly mentored me when I sought them out for advice, and the care and love of the most wonderful girl in the world.

when I am feeling very bad, usually I'll latch onto some song extra hard.

I like this song because it doesn't pretend things are going to be easy.

at some point, it started to feel true.

I'd seen the sun before, but it was different this time. I'd made it through my worst fears, and it hadn't killed me. I could do it again if need be. A bad situation had worked out all right in the end, but even if it hadn't, I would have been okay. I wasn't reaching my expiration date as a young creator—I was maturing, building the strength, real strength, to live the rest of my life.

take a breath,
as well as you
can

and prepare for
the careful climb
down.

you have a long life
still to live

and many more
mountains to climb.

This isn't a resolution, a happy ending—it's the beginning. I will still struggle, and fall, and break, again in the future. There will be highs and lows, and the fire is something I'll have to carefully manage for the rest of my life. But the places I've been broken will not break so easily in the same way again.

It's been a hard year, an ugly year, a long year.
It's been a good year.
On to the next.

2019

it has been a year since it all came crashing down.

my hair is getting pretty long.

each inch is a reminder that I made it this far.

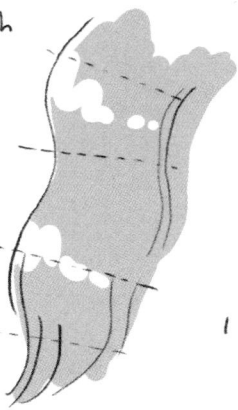

I try not to pull out the strands.

my arms
are getting
stronger.

I try not to
pick the
skin.

I use my lungs
to breathe.

at night
I close
my eyes,

and in the morning I will
open them again.

my flame
burns
soft
& warm.

take a breath,
as well as you can.

turn your face toward
the light.

it is time for the
next step of your journey.

My dad always said we would all get married in the old family church

I never had any feelings about that until I realized I was no longer welcome there.

at first, it was a relief.

like a knot of dread that I had been born with had suddenly unraveled.

but
then

don't laugh, okay?

I thought I'd left all this behind.

I thought I'd been okay with that.

maybe it's okay to want this, after all.

Every cell in my body
has died
and grown again

acknowledgments

To my wife (wife!!) Molly—you are my light in the darkness and an inspiration to me, always. I can't wait for the rest of our lives together.

To Mom and Dad, Grandma and Opa, Alex, Hannah, Gracie, and Jacob—I love you and you'll always be a part of me. Don't let this book make you worry too much!

To Andrew and Charlie—you believed in me before anyone else did. Thank you for giving me this chance to tell my story.

Thank you to Cat San Juan and Erin Fitzsimmons for designing such a beautiful book!

To Aimee, my rock when I was adrift at sea—that salad saved me in more ways than you know.

To the Taylors—you're always in my heart no matter how far apart we are!

To Grace and Nicole—thank you, and I'm sorry.

To Ms. Hendrix, who fought for me to get an arts education even if it meant teaching two classes at the same time—I wouldn't be here without you!

To Team She-Ra—working with you has been the honor of a lifetime. Thank you for defending and believing in me.

To Lacey—thank you for your mentorship that helped me pull through an impossible situation. I couldn't have done it without you.

To all my friends who have given me a listening ear, a shoulder to cry on, or just quiet solidarity—I am so fortunate and grateful to have you in my life and I hope to always be the friend you deserve.

To Winston, Toast, and Fig—you're pets and you can't read, but thank you for your companionship that has comforted me through so many gray skies and cold nights.

To all the fans and readers who have supported me and encouraged me over the past eight years—you can never know how deeply grateful I am to you. You changed my life—thank you so much.

Photos on pages 1, 26, 33, 53, 54, 59, 81, 89, 96, 107, 123, 135, 143, 161, 185, 187 courtesy of the author.

Photo on page 193 courtesy of Jamie Thrower / Studio XIII Photography.

Images on pages 48 and 54 previously appeared in Noelle Stevenson's NIMONA, 2015.

Page 98:
"Second Chance"
By Dame, from the self-titled album "Dame" (c) and (p) Dame 2004 released by Lujo Records
Lyrics reprinted courtesy of Lujo Records

Pages 118-119:
"Friday I'm In Love"
Words and Music by Robert Smith, Simon Gallup, Paul S. Thompson, Boris Williams and Perry Bamonte
Copyright (c) 1992 by Fiction Songs Ltd.
All Rights in the United States and Canada Administered by Universal Music - MGB Songs
International Copyright Secured All Rights Reserved
Reprinted by Permission of Hal Leonard LLC

Pages 121-122:
"Wherever Is Your Heart"
Written by Brandi Carlile, Tim Hanseroth & Phil Hanseroth
Published by Atlas Music Publishing on behalf of Southern Oracle Music LLC (ASCAP)

Page 183:

I CAN SEE CLEARLY NOW

Words and Music by JOHNNY NASH

Copyright (c) 1972 (Renewed) NASHCO MUSIC

All Rights for the World Outside of North America Administered by WARNER CHAPPELL MUSIC, INC.

All Rights Reserved

Used By Permission of ALFRED MUSIC

10/22- 2

OYSTER BAY - EAST NORWICH PUBLIC LIBRARY
OYSTER BAY, N.Y.

MAY 2 4 2021